Stanton, Henry

What you need to know about Sex

Stanton, Henry

What you need to know about Sex

ISBN/EAN: 978-3-86741-262-9
First published in 2010 by Salzwasser-Verlag, Bremen, Germany.

Salzwasser-Verlag (www.salzwasserverlag.de) is an Imprint of Europaeischer Hochschulverlag GmbH & Co KG, Fahrenheitstr. 1, D-28359 Bremen. All rights reserved.

This book is a reproduction of an out of print title and has originally been published in 1922. Because no electronic master copies of this title could be obtained, the publisher had to reuse old copies of the text. We therefore apologize for any possible loss in quality.

Stanton, Henry

What you need to know about Sex

CONTENTS

CHAPTER I SEX	1
CHAPTER II THE TRANSITION FROM CELL TO HUMAN BEING	8
CHAPTER III SEX IN MALE CHILDHOOD (FROM 14 TO 16)	16
CHAPTER IV SEX IN FEMALE CHILDHOOD (FROM 12 TO 14)	22
CHAPTER V SEX IN THE ADOLESCENT MALE (FROM PUBERTY TO MATURITY)	26
CHAPTER VI SEX IN THE ADOLESCENT FEMALE (FROM PUBERTY TO MATURITY)	31
CHAPTER VII SEX IN THE MARRIAGE RELATION THE HUSBAND	39
CHAPTER VIII SEX IN THE MARRIAGE RELATION THE WIFE	41
CHAPTER IX SEX DISEASES	49
CHAPTER X LOVE AND SEX	53

CHAPTER I
SEX

The happiness of all human beings, men and women, depends largely on their rational solution of the sexual problem. Sex and the part it plays in human life cannot be ignored. In the case of animals sex plays a simpler and less complex rôle. It is a purely natural and instinctive function whose underlying purpose is the perpetuation of the species. It is not complicated by the many incidental phenomena which result, in man's case, from psychologic, economic, moral and religious causes. Climate, social conditions, individual modes of life and work, alcohol, wealth and poverty, and other factors affect sexual activity in human beings.

Sexual love, which is practically unknown to the animals, is a special development of the sex urge in the human soul. The deeper purpose of the sex function in human beings, likewise, is procreation, the reproduction of species.

The average man, woman and child should know the essential sex facts in order to be able to deal with the sex problems of life. Of late years there has been a greater diffusion of such knowledge. To a large extent, however, children and adolescents are still taught to look on all that pertains to sex as something shameful and immodest, something not to be discussed. Sex is an "Avoided Subject."

This is fundamentally wrong. Sex affects the very root of all human life. Its activities are not obscene, but Nature's own means to certain legitimate ends. The sex functions, when properly controlled and led into the proper channels, are a most essential and legitimate form of physical self-expression. The veil of secrecy with which they are so often shrouded tends to create an altogether false impression regarding them. This discussion of these "Avoided Subjects," in "Plain English," is intended to give the salient facts regarding sex in a direct, straightforward manner, bearing in mind the true purpose of normal sex activities.

The more we know of the facts of sex, the right and normal part sex activities play in life, and all that tends to abuse and degrade them, the better able we will be to make sex a factor for happiness in our own lives and that of our descendants. Mankind, for its own general good, must desire that reproduction—the real purpose of every sexual function—occur in such a way as to perpetuate its own best physical and mental qualities.

THE LAW OF PHYSICAL LIFE

It is a universal rule of physical life that every individual being undergoes a development which we know as its individual life and which, so far as its physical substance is concerned, ends with death. Death is the destruction of the greater part of this individual organism which, when death ensues, once more becomes lifeless matter. Only small portions of this matter, the germ cells, continue to live under certain conditions which nature has fixed.

The germ cell—as has been established by the microscope—is the tiny cell which in the lowest living organisms as well as in man himself, forms the unit of physical development. Yet even this tiny cell is already a highly organized and perfected thing. It is composed of the most widely differing elements which, taken together, form the so-called protoplasm or cellular substance. And for all life established in nature the cell remains the constant and unchanging form element. It comprises the cell-protoplasm and a nucleus imbedded in it whose substance is known as the nucleoplasm. The nucleus is the more important of the two and, so to say, governs the life of the cell-protoplasm.

The lower one-celled organisms in nature increase by division, just as do the individual cells of a more highly organized, many-celled order of living beings. And in all cases, though death or destruction of the cells is synonymous with the death or destruction of the living organism, the latter in most cases already has recreated itself by reproduction.

We will not go into the very complicated details of the actual process of the growth and division of the protoplasmic cells. It is enough to say that in the case of living creatures provided with more complicated organisms, such as the higher plants, animals and man, the little cell units divide and grow as they do in the case of the lower organisms. The fact is one which shows the intimate inner relationship of all living beings.

THE LADDER OF ORGANIC ASCENT

As we mount the ascending ladder of plant and animal life the unit-cell of the lower organisms is replaced by a great number of individual cells, which have grown together to form a completed whole. In this complete whole the cells, in accordance with the specific purpose for which they are intended, all have a different form and a different chemical composition. Thus it is that in the case of the plants leaves, flowers, buds, bark, branches and stems are formed, and in that of animals skin, intestines, glands, blood, muscles, nerves, brain and the organs of sense. In spite of the complicated nature of numerous organisms we find that many of them still possess the power of reproducing themselves by division or a process of "budding." In the case of certain plants and animals, cell-groups grow together into a so-called "bud," which later detaches itself from the parent body and forms a new individual living organism, as in the case of the polyps or the tubers in plant life.

A tree, for instance, may be grown from a graft which has been cut off and planted in the ground. And ants and bees which have not been fecundated are quite capable of laying eggs out of which develop perfect, well-formed descendants. This last process is called parthenogenesis. It is a process, however, which if carried on through several generations, ends in deterioration and degeneracy. In the case of the higher animals, vertebrates and man, such reproduction is an impossibility.

These higher types of animal life have been provided by nature with special organs of reproduction and reproductive glands whose secretions, when they are projected from the body under certain conditions, reproduce themselves, and increase and develop in such wise that the living organism from which they proceed is reproduced in practically its identical form. Thus it perpetuates the original type. Philosophically it may be said that these cells directly continue the life of the parents, so that death in reality only destroys a part of the individual. Every individual lives again in his offspring.

THE TRUE MISSION OF SEX

This rebirth of the individual in his descendants represents the true mission of sex where the human being is concerned. And reproduction, the perpetuation of the species, underlies all rightful and normal sex functions and activities. The actual physical process of reproduction, the details which initiate reproduction in the case of the human being, it seems unnecessary here to describe. In the animal world, into which the moral equation does not really enter, the facts of conjugation represent a simple and natural working-out of functional bodily laws, usually with a seasonal determination. But where man is concerned these facts are so largely made to serve the purposes of pruriency, so exploited to inflame the imagination in an undesirable and directly harmful way that they can be approached only with the utmost caution.

The intimate fact knowledge necessary in this connection is of a peculiarly personal and sacred nature, and represents information which is better communicated by the spoken than by the printed word. The wise father and mother are those naturally indicated to convey this information to their sons and daughters by word of mouth. By analogy, by fuller development and description of the reproductive processes of plant and animal life on which we have touched, the matter of human procreation may be approached. Parents should stress the point, when trying to present this subject to the youthful mind, that man's special functions are only a detail—albeit a most important one—in nature's vast plan for the propagation of life on earth. This will have the advantage of correcting a trend on the part of the imaginative boy or girl to lay too much stress on the part humanity plays in this great general reproductive scheme. It will lay weight on the fact that the functional workings of reproduction are not, primarily, a source of pleasure, but that—when safeguarded by the institution of matrimony, on which civilized social life is based—they stand for the observance of solemn duties and obligations, duties to church and state, and obligations to posterity. Hence, parents, in talking to their children about these matters should do so in a sober and instructive fashion. The attention of a mother, perhaps, need not be called to this. But fathers may be inclined, in many cases, to inform their sons without insisting that the information they give them is, in the final analysis, intended to be applied to lofty constructive purposes. They may, in their desire to speak *practically*, forget the moral values which should underlie this intimate information. Never should the spirit of levity intrude itself in these intimate personal sex colloquies. Restraint and decency should always mark them.

In making clear to the mind of youth the fact data which initiates and governs reproduction in animal and in human life, the ideal to be cultivated is continence, the refraining from all experimentation undertaken in a spirit of curiosity, until such time as a well-placed affection, sanctioned by the divine blessing, will justify a sane and normal exploitation of physical needs and urges in the matrimonial state. To this end hard bodily and mental work should be encouraged in the youth of both sexes. "Satan finds work for idle hands to do," has special application in this connection, and a chaste and continent youth is usually the forerunner of a happy and contented marriage. And incidentally, a happy marriage is the best guarantee that reproduction, the carrying on of the species, will be morally and physically a success. Here, too, the fact should be strongly stressed that prostitution cannot be justified on any moral grounds. It represents a deliberate ignoring of the rightful function of sex, and the perversion of the sane and natural laws of reproduction. It is in marriage, in the sane and normal activities of that unit of our whole social system—the family—that reproduction develops nature's basic principle of perpetuation in the highest and worthiest manner, in obedience to laws humane and divine.

CHAPTER II
THE TRANSITION FROM CELL TO HUMAN BEING

In the functional processes alluded to in the preceding chapter, the male germ-cell and the female germ-cell unite in a practically equal division of substance. We say "practically" because the maternal and the paternal influences are not equally divided in the offspring. One or the other usually predominates. But, as a general rule, it may be said that in the development of the embryonal life the process of cell division proceeds in such a way that every germ of the child's future organism represents approximately one-half maternal and one-half paternal substance and energy.

In this process lies the true secret of heredity. The inherited energies retain their full measure of power, and all their original quality in the growing and dividing chromosomes (the chromosome is one of the segments into which the chromoplasmic filaments of a cell-nucleus break up just before indirect division). On the other hand, the egg-substance of the female germ-cell, which is assimilated by the chromosomes, and which is turned into *their* substance by the process of organic chemistry, loses its specific plastic vital energy completely. It is in the same way that food eaten by the adult has absolutely no effect on his qualitative organic structure. We may eat ever so many beef-steaks without acquiring any of the characteristics of an ox. And the germ-cell may devour any amount of egg-protoplasma without losing its original paternal energy. As a rule a child inherits as many qualities from its mother as from its father.

DETERMINATION OF SEX

Sex is determined after conception has taken place. At an early stage of the embryo certain cells are set apart. These, later, form the sex glands. Modern research claims to have discovered the secret of absolutely determining sex in the human embryo, but even if these claims are valid they have not as yet met with any general application.

EARLY DEVELOPMENT

Some twelve days after conception, the female ovule or egg, which has been impregnated by the male spermatazoön, escapes from the ovary where it was impregnated, and entering a tube (Fallopian) gradually descends by means of it into the cavity of the womb or uterus. Here the little germ begins to mature in order to develop into an exact counterpart of its parents. In the human being the womb has only a single cavity, and usually develops but a single embryo.

TWINS

Sometimes two ovules are matured at the same time. If fecundated, two embryos instead of one will develop, producing twins. Triplets and quadruplets, the results of the maturing of three or four ovules at the same time, occur more rarely. As many as five children have been born alive at a single birth, but have seldom lived for more than a few minutes.

GESTATION

The development of the ovule in the womb is known as gestation or pregnancy. The process is one of continued cell division and growth, and while it goes on the ovule sticks to the inner wall of the womb. There it is soon enveloped by a mucous membrane, which grows around it and incloses it.

THE EMBRYO

The *Primitive Trace*, a delicate straight line appearing on the surface of the growing layer of cells is the base of the embryonic spinal column. Around this the whole embryo develops in an intricate process of cell division and duplication. One end of the Primitive Trace becomes the head, the other the tail, for every human being has a tail at this stage of his existence. The neck is marked by a slight depression; the body by a swollen center. Soon little buds or "pads" appear in the proper positions. These represent arms and legs, whose ends, finally, split up into fingers and toes. The embryonic human being has been steadily increasing in size, meanwhile. By the fifth week the heart and lungs are present in a rudimentary form, and ears and face are distinctly outlined. During the seventh week the kidneys are formed, and a little later the genital organs. At two months, though sex is not determined as yet, eyes and nose are visible, the mouth is gaping, and the skin can be distinguished. At ten weeks the sexual organs form more definitely, and in the third month sex can be definitely determined.

THE FOETUS

At the end of its fourth month the embryo — now four or five inches long and weighing about an ounce — is promoted. It receives the name of foetus. Hairs appear on the scalp, the eyes are provided with lids, the tongue appears far back in the mouth. The movements of the foetus are plainly felt by the mother. If born at this time it lives but a few minutes. It continues to gain rapidly in weight. By the sixth month the nails are solid, the liver large and red, and there is fluid in the gall bladder. The seventh month finds the foetus from twelve and a half to fourteen inches long, and weighing about fifty-five ounces. It is now well proportioned, the bones of the cranium, formerly flat, are arched. All its parts are well defined, and it can live if born. By the end of the eighth month the foetus has thickened out. Its skin is red and covered by a delicate down; the lower jaw has grown to the same length as the upper one. The convolutions of the brain structure also appear during this month.

PLACENTA AND UMBILICAL CORD

During gestation the unborn infant has been supplied with air and nourishment by the mother. An organ called the *Placenta*, a spongy growth of blood vessels, develops on the inner point of the womb. To this organ the growing foetus is moored by a species of cable, the *Umbilical Cord*. This cord, also made up mainly of blood vessels, carries the blood of the foetus to and from the *Placenta*, absorbing it through the thin walls which separate it from the mother's blood. Only through her blood can the mother influence the child, since the Umbilical Cord contains no nerves. The Umbilical Cord, attached to the body of the child at the navel, is cut at birth, and with the Placenta is expelled from the womb soon after the child has been born. Together with the Placenta it forms a shapeless mass, familiarly known as the "afterbirth," and when it is retained instead of being expelled is apt to cause serious trouble.

CHILDBIRTH OR PARTURITION

At nine month's time the foetus is violently thrust from that laboratory of nature in which it has formed. It is born, and comes into the world as a child. Considering the ordinary size of the generative passages, the expelling of the foetus from the womb would seem impossible. But Nature, during those months in which she enlarged the womb to hold its gradually increasing contents, has also increased the generative passages in size. She has made them soft and distensible, so that an apparent physical impossibility could take place, though it is often accompanied by intense suffering. Modern medical science has made childbirth easier, but the act of childbirth is usually accompanied by more or less suffering. Excessive pain, however, is often the result of causes which proper treatment can remove before and at the time of confinement.

TWILIGHT SLEEP

The so-called "Twilight Sleep," a modern development, by which the pangs of childbirth are obviated by the administration of drugs or by hypnotic suggestion, has its opponents and defenders. The advantage of a painless childbirth, upon which the mother can look back as on a dream, is evident. The "Twilight Sleep" process has been used with the happiest results both for parent and child. Opponents of this system declare that the use of powerful drugs may injure the child. A method commended is the administration of a mixture of laughing gas and oxygen, which relieves the mother and does not affect the child.

THE NEW-BORN INFANT

The average weight of the new-born child is about seven and a half pounds. It is insensitive to pain for the first few days, and seems deaf (since its middle ears are filled with a thick mucus) for the first two weeks. During the first few days, too, it does not seem able to see. The first month of its existence is purely automatic. Evidences of dawning intelligence appear in the second month and at four months it will recognize mother or nurse. Muscularly it is poorly developed. Not until two months old is it able to hold up its head, and not until three months does voluntary muscular movement put in an appearance. The new-born's first self-conscious act is to draw breath. Deprived of its usual means of supply it must breathe or suffocate. Its next is to suck milk, lest it starve.

HEREDITY

We often find children who offer a striking resemblance to a paternal grandfather, a maternal aunt or a maternal great-grandmother. This is known as avatism. There are many curious variations with regard to the inheritance of ancestral traits. Some children show a remarkable resemblance to their fathers in childhood, others to their mothers. And many qualities of certain individual ancestors appear quite suddenly late in life. Everything may be inherited, from the most delicate shadings of the disposition, the intelligence and the will power, to the least details of hair, nails and bone structure, etc. And the combination of the qualities of one's ancestors in heredity is so manifold and so unequal that it is extremely difficult to arrive at fixed conclusions regarding it. Hereditary traits and tendencies are developed out of the energies of the original conjugated germ-cells throughout life, up to the very day of death. Even aged men often show peculiarities in the evening of their life which may be clearly recognized as inherited, and duplicating others shown by their forbears at the same period of life.

As has already been mentioned every individual inherits, generally speaking, as much from his paternal as from his maternal progenitors. This in spite of the fact that the tiny paternal germ-cell is the only medium of transmission of the paternal qualities, while the mother furnishes the much larger egg-cell, and feeds him throughout the embryonic period.

THE ENGRAM

An interesting theory maintains that the external impressions made upon an organism which reacts to them and receives them, might be called *engrams* or "inscriptions." Thus the impression of some object we have seen or touched (let us say we have seen a lion) may remain engraved on our mind as an impression. Hence every memory picture is one of engrams, whether the impression is a conscious one or an unconscious one. According to this same theory the reawakening of an older impression is an *ecphory*. Some new stimulation may thus ecphorate an old engram. Now the entire embryonal development of the human child is in reality no more than a continuous process of ecphoration of old engrams, one after another. And the entire complex of our living human organism is made up entirely of these energy-complexes engraved on our consciousness or subconsciousness. The sum total of all these engrams, in a living human being, according to the theory advanced, is given the name of *mnema*. That which the child receives in the way of energies contained in the germ-cells from its ancestors is his hereditary *mnema*. And that which he acquires in the course of his own individual life is his acquired or individual *mnema*.

CHAPTER III
SEX IN MALE CHILDHOOD
(FROM 14 TO 16)

During the first years of child life all those laws of practical hygiene which make for good health should be carefully observed. Every organ of the body should be carefully protected, even at this early age. The genital organs, especially, should not be rubbed or handled under any pretext, beyond what is absolutely necessary for cleanliness. The organs of generation, which we are apt to treat as nonexistent in children, just because they are children, claim just as much watchful care as any others.

SEX PRECAUTIONS IN INFANCY

Even in infancy, the diaper should fit easily about the organs which it covers, so as not to give rise to undue friction or heating of the parts. And for the same reason it should always be changed immediately after urination or a movement of the bowels. No material which prevents the escape of perspiration, urine or fecal matter should be employed for a diaper. The use of a chair-commode as early as the end of the first year is highly to be commended, as being more comfortable for the sex organs and healthier for the child. It favors, in particular, a more perfect development of limbs and hip joints.

EARLY SEX IMPRESSIONS

Sex impressions and reactions are apt to develop at an early age, especially in the case of boys. If the child's physical health is normal, however, they should not affect his mind or body. The growing boy should be encouraged to take his sex questions and sex problems to his parents (in his case preferably the father) for explanation. Thus they may be made clear to him naturally and logically. He should not be told what he soon discovers is not true: that babies are "dug up with a silver spade," or make their appearances in the family thanks to the kind offices of storks or angels. Instead, by analogy with the reproductive processes of all nature, the true facts of sex may be explained to him in a soothing and normal way.

EVIL COMMUNICATIONS

Too often, the growing boy receives his first lessons regarding sex from ignorant and vicious associates. Curiosity is one of the greatest natural factors in the child's proper development, if rightly directed. When wrongly led, however, it may have the worst consequences. Even before puberty occurs, a boy's attention may be quite naturally drawn to his own sex organs.

NATURAL CAUSES OF INFANT SEXUAL PRECOCITY

Sexual precocity in boys may be natural or it may be artificially called forth. Among natural causes which develop sex precocity is promiscuous playing with other boys and girls for hours without supervision. It may also be produced by playful repose on the stomach, sliding down banisters, going too long without urinating, by constipation or straining at stool, irritant cutaneous affections, and rectal worms. Sliding down banisters, for instance, produces a titillation. The act may be repeated until inveterate masturbation results, even at an early age. Needless laving, handling and rubbing of the private parts is another natural incitement to sexual precocity.

PRIAPISM

Priapism is a disease which boys often develop. It may be either a result or a cause of sexual precocity, and may come from undue handling of the genital parts or from a morbid state of health. It takes the form of paroxysms, more or less frequent, and of violent and often painful erection, calling for a physician's attention. If the result of a functional disorder, and not arrested, it is in danger of giving rise to masturbation. This morbid condition sometimes seriously impairs the health.

MASTURBATION

Masturbation, the habit of self-abuse, often formed before puberty, is an artificial development of sexual precocity. Most boys, from the age of nine to fourteen, interest themselves in sex questions and matters, but these are usually presented to them in a lewd and improper manner, by improperly informed companions. Dwelling upon these thoughts the boy is led to play with his sex organs in secret and masturbation results. A secret vice of the most dangerous kind, masturbation or self-pollution is often taught by older boys and takes place, to quote an authority "in many of our colleges, boarding, public and private schools," and is also indulged in by companions beneath the home roof. If it becomes habitual, generally impaired health, and often epilepsy, and total moral and physical degradation results. Stains on the nightshirt or sheet occurring before puberty are absolute evidence of the vice in boys.

WHAT FATHERS SHOULD DO FOR THEIR BOYS

Make sex facts clear to your boy as interesting, matter-of-fact developments of general natural laws. Ungratified or improperly gratified curiosity is what leads to a young boy's overemphasizing the facts of sex as they apply to him. Make him your confidant. Teach him to think cleanly and to act cleanly, neither to ignore nor to exalt the sexual. Especially, when he himself is directly disturbed sexually, either in a mental or physical way, let him feel that he can apply to you naturally for relief and explanation. If this be done, your boy's sex development before puberty will be natural and normal, and when the more serious and difficult problems of adolescence present themselves, he will be prepared to handle them on the basis of right thinking and right living. Natural and healthy sport in the open air, and the avoidance of foul language and indecency should be stressed. The use of alcohol, coffee and tea by children tends to weaken their sexual organs. Every boy should know that chastity means continence. He should know that lascivious thoughts lead to lascivious actions, and that these are a drain on his system which may spoil his life in later years.

In the education of his children the average man is only too apt to repeat the same mistake of unconsciously crediting the child with the possession of his own feelings and his own outlook, that is the feelings and outlook of the adult. In general, things which may make an impression in a sex way on the adult are a matter of indifference to the sexually unripe boy. Hence it is quite possible for a father to discuss sex matters with his young son and inform him constructively, without in any undue way rousing his sex curiosity or awakening desire. Such talks, of course, should be in accordance with the principles already laid down in the section on "Reproduction."

If a boy is accustomed and taught to regard sex conditions and matters in a proper and innocent manner, as something perfectly natural, improper curiosity and eroticism are far less likely to be aroused than when this is not the case. For the whole subject will have lost the dangerous attraction of novelty. On the other hand, we find boys who have been brought up with great prudery and in complete ignorance of sex matters (save that which may come to them from impure sources) greatly excited and ashamed by the first appearance of the indications of puberty. Secrecy is the enemy of a clean, normal conception on the part of the child as to the right place sex and the sex function play in life and in the world. It stands to reason, of course, that every least detail of the sex question cannot be intelligently made clear to a little child. But his questions should all be answered, honestly, and with due regard for his age and his capacity to understand what is explained to him.

One very great advantage of an early paternal explanation of sex matters to the boy is its beneficial effect on the mind and the nerves. Many boys brood or grow melancholy when confronted with sex riddles and problems for which they are unable to find a solution; and as the result of totally erroneous ideas they may have formed with regard to sex matters. At the same time too much attention should not be paid the discussion of sex questions between father and son. A father should, so far as possible, endeavor to develop other interests and preoccupations in his boy, and turn his mind as much as may be *away* from matters sexual, until the age when the youth is ripe for marriage is reached.

CHAPTER IV
SEX IN FEMALE CHILDHOOD
(FROM 12 TO 14)

What has been said in general about practical observance of the laws of sex hygiene in the preceding chapter for boys, applies to girls as well. If anything the sex precautions taken in infancy should be even more closely followed, as girls are by nature less robust than boys. If children could be raised in entire accordance with natural laws, the sexual instinct of girls as well as boys would probably remain dormant during the period stretching from infancy to puberty. As in the case of the boy, so in that of the girl, any manifestation of sexual precocity should be investigated, to see whether it be due to natural or artificial causes. In either case the proper remedies should be applied.

SEX PRECOCITY IN GIRLS

There are cases of extraordinary sex precocity in girls. One case reported in the United States was that of a female child who at birth possessed all the characteristics usually developed at puberty. In this case the natural periodical changes began at birth! Fortunately, this is a case more or less unique. In little girls and boys undue sexual handling or titillating of their genital organs tends to quiet them, so nurses (let us hope in ignorance of the consequences!) often resort to it. Sending children to bed very early, to "get rid of them," or confining them in a room by themselves, tends to encourage the development of vicious habits. A single bed, both in the school and in the home, is indispensable to purity of morals and personal cleanliness. It tends to restrain too early development of the sexual instinct both in small girls and small boys.

SEXUAL SELF-ABUSE IN GIRLS

Small girls, like small boys, display an intelligent curiosity as regards the phenomena of sex at an early age. And what has already been said regarding its improper gratification in the preceding chapter, so far as boys are concerned, applies with equal force to them. In their case, however, the mother is a girl's natural confidant and friend. Self-abuse in one or another form is as common in the case of the girl as in that of the boy. As a rule, girls who live an outdoor life, and work with their muscles more than their mind, do not develop undue precocious sexual curiosities or desires. At least they do not do so to the same extent as those more nervously and susceptibly constituted. The less delicate and sensitive children of the country tend less to these habits than their more sensitively organized city brothers and sisters. Girls who have formed vicious habits are apt to indulge in the practice of self-abuse at night when going to bed. If there is cause for suspicion, the bedclothes should be quickly and suddenly thrown off under some pretense. Self-abuse usually has a marked effect on the genital organs of girls. The inner organs become unnaturally enlarged and distended, and *leucorrhea*, catarrh of the vagina, attended by a discharge of greenish-white mucus, often develops.

RESULTS OF SELF-ABUSE IN GIRLS

Local diseases, due to this cause, result in girls as well as boys. Temporary congestions become permanent, and develop into permanent irritations and disorders. Leucorrhea has already been mentioned. Contact with the acrid, irritating internal secretions also causes *soreness of the fingers at the root of the nails*, and warts. Congestion and other diseases are other ultimate results of the habit; and these congestions to which it gives rise unduly hasten the advent of puberty. Any *decided enlargement of the labia and clitoris in a young girl* may be taken as a positive evidence of the existence of the habit of self-abuse. Sterility, and atrophy of the breasts—their deficient development—when the vice is begun before puberty, is another result.

PRURITIS AND FEMININE NOCTURNAL EMISSIONS

Pruritis (itching genitals), though not necessarily caused by self-abuse, may be one of its consequences. Continued congestion causes the genital parts to itch terribly. This itching increases until the desire to manipulate the genitals becomes irresistible. It will then be indulged in even in the presence of strangers, though the girl in question at other times may be exceptionally modest. Girls addicted to the vice also suffer from nocturnal emissions. The general effect of self-abuse is much the same in the case of a girl as in that of a boy, for leucorrhea is injurious in somewhat the same fashion as seminal loss. In the case of girls the greatest injury, however, is due to the nervous exhaustion which succeeds the unnatural excitement.

WHAT MOTHERS SHOULD DO FOR THEIR GIRLS

A healthy girl should be happy and comfortable in all respects. She will not be so, especially with regard to her sex problems, unless she can appeal to her mother as a friend and confidant. While keeping your girl's mind pure and healthy by precept and example, do not forget that the best way to protect her against evil influences and communications is to tell her the exact truth about sex facts, as they apply to her, just as the father should his boy. Keep your girl fully occupied and do not leave her sex education to the evil winds of chance.

Let sex knowledge take its place as a proper, necessary part of her general education. If your daughter feels she can at all times talk freely to you all will be well. Gratify her natural sex curiosity in a natural way. See that *immediate* medical attention is given inflammations, excoriations, itchings and swellings of her genital organs. Such conditions will lead her to rub and scratch these parts—never to be touched—for relief. If, as a result of the sensations experienced, masturbation results, *yours is the sin*.

CHAPTER V
SEX IN THE ADOLESCENT MALE
(FROM PUBERTY TO MATURITY)

Adolescence is the period when the boy is lost in the man. It is the time of life embraced between the ages of fourteen or sixteen and the age of twenty-five. Every boy, if properly trained, should reach this period in a state of good general health and spirits. Hitherto he has been led and guided. Now he must develop mental strength and will power himself to choose the good and refuse the evil in the sexual problems confronting him.

PUBERTY

According to climate puberty, the age when the human male becomes sexually perfect, varies from ten to fifteen years. In the United States puberty in the male usually occurs at the age of fourteen and a half years. In tropical climates it occurs at nine or ten, and in cold countries, such as Norway and Siberia, it may not take place until eighteen or nineteen. Vigorous physical exercise tends to delay puberty, anything exciting the emotions tends to hasten it. Stimulating foods, pepper, vinegar, mustard, spices, tea and coffee, excess meat nutriment hasten puberty. A cool, unstimulating vegetable and farinaceous diet may delay the development of the sexual system several months or a year.

THE SIGNS AND CHANGES OF PUBERTY

In the boy the signs of puberty are the growth of hair on the skin covering the pubes and in the armpits. Chest and arms broaden, the frame grows more angular, the masculine proportions more pronounced. The vocal cords grow longer and lower the pitch of the voice. Hair grows on chin, upper lip, cheeks, and often on the body surface.

THE SEXUAL MORAL LAW

The sexual moral law is the same for both sexes, and equally binding. It may be summed up as follows: "Your sexual urges, instincts and desires should never consciously injure an individual human being or mankind in general. They should be exercised to further the value and happiness of both."

THE MALE ADOLESCENT AND CONTINENCE

The perfect carrying out of this general moral law implies continence on the part of the male adolescent until marriage. Continence is positive restraint under all circumstances. Strict continence is neither injurious to health, nor does it produce impotence. While self-denial is difficult, since the promptings of nature often seem imperious, it is not impossible. It is certain that no youth will suffer, physically, by remaining sexually pure. The demands which occur during adolescence are mainly abnormal, due to the excitements of an overstimulating diet, pornographic literature and art, and the temptations of impure association.

WHY YOUNG MEN GO WRONG

Foul thoughts, once they enter the mind, corrode it. The sensual glance, the bawdy laugh, the ribald jest, the smutty story, the obscene song may be met with on street corner, in the car, train, hotel lobby, lecture hall and workshop. Mental unchastity ends in physical unchastity. The habit common to most adolescent boys and young men of relating smutty stories, repeating foul jokes and making indecent allusions destroys respect for virtue. In addition there are such direct physical causes of undue adolescent sexual excitement as constipation and alcoholism, and such mental ones as nervous irritability.

To the constant discussion and speculation regarding sex and its mysteries by the adolescent young male, must be added the artificial idea that idle prattling on the subject is a sign of "manhood." Thus many young men whose natural trend is in the direction of decency and right sexual living, "step out" or "go to see the girls," as the phrase is, because they think that otherwise "they are not real men." More subtle in its evil effect, yet somewhat less dangerous physically, perhaps, than the professional prostitute is the lure of the "hidden" prostitute, who carefully conceals her derelictions, and publicly wraps herself in a mantle of virtue.

PROSTITUTION

The training of the average male mind in impure language and thought during boyhood and adolescence, the cultivation of his animal at the expense of the moral nature, often leads the adolescent to seek satisfaction by frequenting the prostitute.

Prostitution, known as the "social evil," is promiscuous unchastity for gain. It has existed in all civilized countries from earliest times. Prostitution abuses the instinct for reproduction, the basic element of sex, to offer certain women a livelihood which they prefer to other means. Love of excitement, inherited criminal propensities, indolence and abnormal sex appetite are first causes of prostitution. Difficulty in finding work, laborious and ill-paid work, harsh treatment of girls at home, indecent living among the poor, contact with demoralizing companions, loose literature and amusements are secondary causes. They all contribute to debauch male and female youth and lead it to form dangerous habits of vicious sensual indulgence.

Prostitution seems inseparable from human society in large communities. The fact is acknowledged in the name given it, "the necessary evil." Regulation and medical control only arrest in a degree the spread of venereal diseases to which prostitution gives rise. The elementary laws on which prostitution rests seems to be stronger than the artificial codes imposed by moral teaching. It is an evil which must be combatted *individually*. Men are principally responsible, in one way or another, for the existence of the social evil. In the case of the young man, abstention is the only cure for the probable results of indulging his animal passions by recourse to the prostitute.

Prostitution, both public and private is the most dangerous menace to society at large. It is the curse of individual young manhood because of the venereal diseases it spreads. One visit to a house of prostitution may ruin a young man's health and life, and millions of human beings die annually from the effects of poison contracted in these houses. "Wild oats" sown in company with the prostitute usually bear fruit in the shape of the most loathsome and destructive sex disorders.

The development of self-control, the avoidance of impure thoughts and associations, the cultivation of the higher moral nature instead of the lower animal one, and, finally, *marriage*, should prevent the young man from falling into prostitution. All the state and medical regulation in the world will not protect him from the venereal diseases he is so apt to acquire by such indulgence.

FREE LOVE

Free love is the doctrine of *unrestrained choice, without binding ties*, in sexual relations. For altogether different reasons, however, it is quite as objectionable as prostitution for the young man. It may offer better hygienic guarantees. But it is a sexual partnership which is opposed to the fundamental institution of *marriage*, on which society in general is based throughout the world. And, aside from the fact that it is a promiscuous relationship not sanctioned by law or society, it is seldom practically successful. It cannot admit of true love without bitter jealousies.

CHAPTER VI
SEX IN THE ADOLESCENT FEMALE
(FROM PUBERTY TO MATURITY)

Adolescence in the girl is the period when she develops into a woman. It is that stage in female life embraced between the ages of twelve or fourteen and twenty-one years. Elasticity of body, a clear complexion, and a happy control of her feelings should mark the young girl at this time, if she has been so fortunate as to escape the dangers and baneful influences of childhood and infancy. Her numerous bodily functions should be well performed. Thus constituted she should be in a condition to take up her coming struggle with the world, and the sex problem it will present.

PUBERTY

It has been noticed that in the case of girls, puberty usually occurs earlier in brunettes than in blondes. In general, it makes its appearance earlier in those of a nervous or bilio-nervous temperament than in those whose temperament is phlegmatic or lymphatic. In the United States fourteen and a half years is the usual age of puberty in girls. In tropical lands, however, it is not uncommon for a girl to be a mother at twelve. Country girls (and boys) usually mature several months or a year later than those living in cities. Too early a puberty in girls may well arouse concern. It usually indicates some inherent constitutional weakness. Premature puberty is often associated with premature decay.

THE SIGNS AND CHANGES OF PUBERTY

In the girl the sign of puberty is the growth of hair about the pubes, private organs and armpits. Her whole frame remains more slender than in the male. Muscles and joints are less prominent, limbs more rounded and tapering. Internal and external organs undergo rapid enlargement, locally. The *mammæ* (the breasts) enlarge, the ovaries dilate, and a periodical uteral discharge (menstruation) is established.

MENSTRUATION

No young girl should feel alarmed if, owing to the negligence of her parents or guardians to prepare her, she is surprised by this first flow from the genital organs. Puberty is the proper time for the appearance of menstruation. This is the periodical development and discharge of an ovule (one or more) by the female, accompanied by the discharge of a fluid, known as menses or catamenia. Menstruation, in general good health, should occur about every twenty-eight days, or once in four weeks. This rule, however, is subject to great variation. Menstruation continues from puberty to about the forty-fifth year, which usually marks the *menopause*, or "change of life." When it disappears a woman is no longer capable of bearing children. Her period of fertility has passed. In rare cases menstruation has stopped at 35, or lasted till 60.

HINTS FOR OBSERVANCE DURING MENSTRUATION

When the period arrives a girl or woman has a feeling of discomfort and lassitude, there is a sense of weight, and a disclination for society. Menstruation should not, however, be regarded as a nuisance; a girl's friends respect her most when she is "unwell." She should keep more than usually quiet while the flow continues, which it will do for a few days. Also, she should avoid all unnecessary fatigue, exposure to wet or to extremes of temperature. Some girls are guilty of the crime of trying to arrest the menstruation flow, and resorting to methods of stopping it. Why? In order to attend a dance or pleasure excursion! Lives have been lost by thus suppressing the monthly flux. Mothers should instruct their daughters when the menses are apt to begin, and what their function is. During menstruation great care must be taken in using water internally. A chill is sufficient to arrest the flow. If menstruation does not establish itself in a healthy or normal manner at the proper time, consult a physician in order to remove this abnormal condition. Any disturbance of the delicate menstrual functions during the period, by constrained positions, muscular effort, brain work and mental or physical excitement, is apt to have serious consequences.

CONTINENCE AND THE YOUNG ADOLESCENT GIRL

Continence is, as a rule more easily observed by the adolescent girl than by the adolescent youth. Ordinarily the normal young girl has no *undue* sexual propensities, amorous thoughts or feelings. Though she is exposed to the danger of meeting other girls who may be lewd in thought and speech, in the houses of friends or at school, she is not apt to be carried away by their example. Yet even a good, pure-minded young girl may be debauched. Especially during adolescence, the easy observance of natural continence depends greatly on the proper functioning of the feminine genital organs. These may be easily disturbed. The syringe used for injections, for so-called purposes of cleanliness, is in reality a danger. The inner organs are self-cleansing. Water or other fluids cast into them disorder the mucous follicles, and dry up their secretions, preventing the flowing out of some of Nature's necessities. A daily washing of the inner organs for a long period with water also produces chronic leucorrhea.

WHY YOUNG GIRLS FALL

Lack of proper early training, abnormal sex instincts, weak good nature, poverty, all may be responsible for a young girl's moral downfall. As a general thing, right home training and home environment, and sane sex education will prevent the normally good girl from going wrong. It should be remembered, though, that a naturally more gentle and yielding disposition may easily lead her into temptation. Girls who are sentimentally inclined should beware of giving way to advances on the part of young men which have only one object in view: the gratification of their animal passion.

The holding of hands and similar innocent beginnings often pave the way for more familiar caresses. Passionate kisses—the promiscuous kiss, by the way, may be the carrier of that dread infection, syphilis—violently awaken a young girl's sex instincts. The fact is that many innocent girls idealize their seducers. They believe their lying promises, actually come to love them, and think that in gratifying their inflamed desires, they are giving a proof of the depth and purity of their own affection.

Here, as in the case of the young man, self-control should be the first thing cultivated. And self-control should be made doubly sure by never permitting one of the opposite sex to show undue familiarity. Many a seemingly innocent flirtation, begun with a kiss, has ended in shame and disgrace, in loss of social standing and position, venereal disease, or even death. The pure-minded and innocent girl often becomes a victim of her ignorance of the consequences entailed by giving in to the desires of some male companion. *The girl who has a knowledge of sex facts is less apt to be taken advantage of in this manner.*

MODERN CONDITIONS WHICH ENCOURAGE IMMORALITY

Excessive Freedom.—The excessive freedom granted the young girl, especially since the World War, must be held responsible for a great increase in familiarity between the adolescent youth of both sexes. Many young girls of the "flapper" type, in particular, are victims of these conditions of unrestrained sex association. Sex precocity is furthered in coeducational colleges, in the high school and the home. Adolescents of both sexes too often are practically unhampered in their comings and goings, their words and actions. The surreptitious pocket flask, filled with "hooch," is often a feature of social parties, dances and affairs frequented by young people. Girls and boys drink together, and as alcohol weakens moral resistance in the one case, and stimulates desire in the other, deplorable consequences naturally result. In the United States the number of girls "sent home" from colleges, and of high-school girls being privately treated by physicians to save them from disgrace, is incredibly large.

Parents who do not control the social activities of their daughters, who permit them to spend their evenings away from home with only a general idea of what they are doing or whom they are meeting, need not be surprised if their morals are undermined.

The Auto.—The advent of the automobile is responsible for an easy and convenient manner of satisfying precociously aroused sex instincts in young girls and boys. Often, unconscientious pleasure-seekers roam the roads in their auto. They accost girls who are walking and offer them a "lift." When the latter refuse to gratify their desires they are often beaten and flung from the car. The daily press has given such publicity to this civilized form of "head hunting," that it is difficult to sympathize with girls who are thus treated. They cannot help but know that in nine cases out of ten, a stranger who invites them to a ride, who "picks" them up, does so with the definite purpose already mentioned in view.

Poverty.—Poverty, too, plays a large part in driving young girls into a life of vice. In all our large cities there are hundreds of young women who earn hardly enough to buy food and fuel and pay for the rent of a room in a cheap lodging house. Feminine youth longs for dress, for company, for entertainment. It is easy enough to find a "gentleman friend" who will provide all three, in exchange for "companionship." So the bargain is struck. These conditions exist in a hundred and one occupations. A young woman may go to a large city as pure as snow, but finding no lucrative employment, lonely and despondent, she is led to take her first step on the downward path. Soon daily contact with vice removes abhorrence to it. Familiarity makes it habitual, and another life is ruined. The heartless moral code of the cynical young pleasure-seeking male is summed up in the cant phrase anent women: "Find, ... and forget!" It is these girls, who are victimized by their lack of self-restraint or moral principle, their ignorance or weakness, who make possible the application of such a maxim.

VIRGINITY

Both mental and physical purity are rightfully required of the young girl about to marry. How shall she acquire and maintain this desirable state of purity? The process is a simple one. *She must let a knowledge of the true hygienic and moral laws of her sex guide her in her relations with men.* She must cultivate clean thought on a basis of physical cleanliness. She need not be ignorant to be pure. Men she should study carefully. She should not allow them to sit with their arm about her waist, to hold her hand, to kiss her. No approach nor touch beyond what the best social observance sanctions should be permitted. Even the tendernesses and familiarities of courtship should be restrained. An engagement does not necessarily culminate in a marriage, and once the foot has slipped on virtue's path the error cannot be recalled. These considerations, together with those adduced in the preceding section, "Why Young Girls Fall," are well worth taking to heart by every young woman who wishes to approach matrimony in the right and proper way.

CHAPTER VII
SEX IN THE MARRIAGE RELATION
THE HUSBAND

Marriage is the process by which a man and woman enter into a complete physical, legal and moral union. The natural object of marriage is the complete community of life for the establishment of a family.

THE MARRIAGEABLE AGE AND ADAPTATION

At twenty-four the male body attains its complete development; and twenty-five is a proper age for the young man to marry. Romantic love, personal affection on a basis of congeniality, mutual adaptation, a similar social sphere of life, should determine his choice. Nature and custom indicate that the husband should be somewhat older than the wife.

MEN WHO SHOULD NOT MARRY

Men suffering with diseases which may be communicated by contagion or heredity should not marry. These diseases include: tuberculosis, syphilis, cancer, leprosy, epilepsy and some nervous disorders, some skin diseases and insanity. A worn-out rake has no business to marry, since marriage is not a hospital for the treatment of disease, or a reformatory institution for moral lepers. Those having a marked tendency to disease must not marry those of similar tendency. The marriage of cousins is not to be advocated. The blood relation tends to bring together persons with similar morbid tendencies. Where both are healthy, however, there seems to be no special liability to mental incompetency, though such marriages are accused of producing defective or idiot children. Men suffering from congenital defects should not marry. Natural blindness, deafness, muteness, and congenital deformities of limb are more or less likely to be passed on to their children. There are cases of natural blindness, though, to which this rule does not apply. Criminals, alcoholics, and persons disproportionate in size should not marry. In the last-mentioned, lack of mutual physical adaptability may produce much unhappiness, especially on the part of the wife. Serious local disease, sterility, and great risk in childbirth may result. Disparity of years, disparity of race, a poverty which will not permit the proper raising of children, undesirable moral character are all good reasons for not marrying.

MEDICAL EXAMINATION BEFORE MARRIAGE

Medical examination as a preliminary to marriage is practically more valuable than a marriage license. Since many entirely innocent young girls today suffer from disease, incurred either through hereditary or accidental infection, a would-be husband may be said to be quite as much entitled to protection as his bride-to-be. Prohibitive physical defects are also discovered in this connection.

CHAPTER VIII
SEX IN THE MARRIAGE RELATION
THE WIFE

Girls marry, in the final analysis, because love for the male is an innate natural principle of the female nature. At its best this love is pure and chaste. The good woman realizes that its first purpose is not mere carnal pleasure. It is a special avowal of the wife's relations to her husband, and its natural as well as moral end is the establishment of the family on the basis of a healthy progeny.

BEFORE MARRIAGE

The wife-to-be, like her prospective husband, will be well advised to ask for a medical health certificate. No man, no matter how good his reputation may be, should marry (on his own account as well as that of the girl) without thorough examination by a physician. The consequences of venereal infection administered to unborn children by their parents are too horrible to allow of any risk being taken. Another bit of advice, which cannot be too highly commended, is that the prospective husband and wife, before they marry, have a plain talk with each other regarding individual sexual peculiarities and needs. A heart-to-heart talk of this kind would be apt to prevent great disappointments and incompatibilities which otherwise may become permanent.

THE WIFE AND HER POSITION

The natural instinct of a man is to seek his mate. On her he depends for an orderly and lawful indulgence of his sex demands. The greatest longevity and best health are to be found among happily married fathers and mothers. No young woman should marry without a full knowledge of her sex duties to her husband. And she should never consummate the marriage vow grudgingly.

CHILDBIRTH HYGIENE

Childbirth is the natural consequence of marriage. Its processes have already been explained in Chapter II of this book. There are, however, some hygienic facts in connection with it which should be noted. Once pregnancy is established, as soon as the fact is suspected, the mother-to-be should look on the little embryo as already a member of the family. Every act of each parent should now be performed (at least to some degree) with reference to the forthcoming infant. The mother's thoughts should be directed to it as much as possible. Mentally she should read literature of a lofty and ennobling character. The theory is that this serves a good purpose in producing a more perfect, healthy and intelligent child. Physically, she should take plenty of active exercise during gestation. Active exercise does not, of course, mean violent exercise. And she should use a "Health Lift." During this time she should subsist as far as possible on a farinaceous diet, fruits and vegetables. The foods should be plainly cooked, without spices. If all else is as it should be, the birth of the child at the end of the customary nine months will be attended by comparatively little pain and danger.

HOW OFTEN SHOULD CHILDBIRTH TAKE PLACE?

It is most important that the childbearing wife and mother have a long period of rest between births. At least one year should separate a birth and the conception following it. This means that about two years should elapse between two births. If this rule be followed, the wife will retain her health, and her children will also be healthy. It is far better to give birth to seven children, who will live and be healthy, than to bear fourteen, of whom seven are likely to die, while the numerous successive births wear out and age the unfortunate mother.

MATRIMONIAL ADJUSTMENT

The above paragraph deals with one detail of what might be called "matrimonial adjustment." This adjustment or compromise is a feature of all successful marriages. The individual cravings of husband and wife must be reconciled by mutual good will and forbearance if they are to be happy. Attention should be paid in particular to not allowing habit, "the worst foe of married happiness," to become too well established in the home, and to cultivate that love and affection which survives the decline of the sexual faculties.

THE IDEAL MARRIAGE

The ideal marriage is the one in which affection combines to bring happiness to both partners in a sane union of sex and soul. As one commentator has rather unhappily expressed it: "When married the *battle* for one united and harmonious life really begins!" It is, indeed, but too often a *battle*! Forbearance, consideration and respect must be the foundation on which the ideal married state is built. The husband should realize that his wife's love for him induces her to allow privileges of a personal nature which her innate chastity and timidity might otherwise refuse. In return, he should accept these privileges with consideration. He should, in particular, on his wedding night, take care not to shock his young bride's sensibilities. He may easily give her a shock from which she will not recover for years, and lead her to form an antipathy against the very act which is "the bond and seal of a truly happy married life."

BIRTH CONTROL

Material changes have taken place in the birthrate of a number of countries during the past fifteen or twenty years which cannot be attributed to purely economic causes. They do not seem to depend on such things as trade, employment and prices; but on the spread of an idea or influence whose tendency must be deplored, that of "birth control," a phrase much heard in these days.

The fact that a decline in human fertility and a falling birth rate are most noticeable in the relatively prosperous countries is a proof that it does not proceed from economic causes; but is due rather to the spread of the doctrine that it is permissible to restrict or control birth. In such countries as the United States, England and Australasia, where the standards of human comfort and living are notoriously high, the decline in the birth rate has been most noticeable. On the other hand, we find perhaps the greatest decline in the birth rate in France, a country where the general well-being probably reaches a lower depth in the community than in any other part of Europe. A comparison of the birth rates of France and of Ireland, for example, offer a valuable illustration of the point under consideration. In France, more than half the women who have reached the age of nubility are married; in Ireland, generally speaking, less than a third. In both countries the crude birth rate is far below that in other European lands. Yet the fertility of the Irish wife exceeded that of her French compeer by 44 per cent in 1880, and by no less than 84 per cent in 1900. And since that time the prolificity of the Irish mother has so increased that she is now, approximately speaking, inferior only to the Dutch or Finnish mother in this respect.

In general, in any country where we find a diminished prolificity a falling off of childbirth *unaccompanied* by a decrease in the number of marriages occurring at the reproductive ages, we may attribute this decrease to *voluntary restriction of childbearing* on the part of the married, or in other words, to the prevalance of "birth control." This incidentally, is not a theoretical statement, but one supported by the almost unanimous medical opinion in all countries. Everywhere and especially here in our own United States, we find evidence of the extensive employ of "birth control" measures to prevent that normal development of family life which underlies the vigor and racial power of every nation. These preventive measures which arbitrarily control human birth had long been in use in France with results which, especially since the war, have been frequently and publicly deplored in the press, and have led the French Government to offer substantial rewards to encourage the propagation of large families. From France the preventive practises of "birth control" had spread, after 1870, over nearly all the countries of western Europe, to England and to the United States; though they are not as much apparent in those countries where the Roman Church has a strong hold on the people.

As a general thing, the practice of thus unnaturally limiting families—"unnaturally" since the custom of "birth control" derives from no natural, physical law—prevails, in the first instance, among the well-to-do, who should rather be the first to set the example of protest against it by having the families they are so much better able to support and educate than those less favored with the world's goods. If the evil of voluntary control of human birth were restricted to a privileged class, say one of wealth, the harm done would, perhaps, not be so great. But, unfortunately, in the course of time it filters down as a "gospel of comfort"—erroneous term!—to those whose resources are less. They accept and practice this invidious system of prevention and gradually the entire community is more or less affected.

The whole system of "birth control" is opposed to natural, human and religious law. Nature, in none of her manifestations, introduces anything which may tend to prevent her great reason for being—the propagation of the species. Birth as the natural sequence of mating is her solemn and invariable law. It is in birth and rebirth that nature renews herself and all the life of the animal and vegetable world, and her primal aim is to encourage it. Human law recognizes this underlying law of nature by forbidding man to tamper in a preventive way with her hallowed and mysterious processes for perpetuating the human race. Religious law, based on the divine dispensation of the Scriptures, indorses the law of nature and that of the state.

We may take it, then, that "birth control" represents a deliberate and reprehensible attempt to nullify those innate laws of reproduction sanctioned by religion, tradition and man's own ingrained instinct. To say that the human instinct for the perpetuation of his race and family has become atrophied during the flight of time, and that he is therefore justified in denying it, is merely begging the question. The instinct may be denied, just as other higher and nobler instincts are disregarded; but its validity cannot be questioned. Whether those who practice "birth control" are influenced by economic, selfishly personal or other reasons, they are offending in a threefold manner: against the inborn wish and desire which is a priceless possession of even the least of God's creatures, that of living anew in its offspring; against the law of the state, which after all, stands for the crystallization of the best feeling of the community; and against the divine injunction handed down to us in Holy Writ, to "increase and multiply."

"Birth control" is the foe to the direct end and aim of marriage, which, in the last analysis, is childbirth. As an enemy to the procreation of children it is an enemy of the family and the family group. As an enemy of the family, it is an enemy of the state, the community, a foe to the whole social system. Mankind has been able to attain its comparatively recent state of moral and physical advancement without having recourse to the dangerous principle which "birth control" represents. Surely that wise provision of our existing legal code which makes the printing or dessimation of information regarding the physical facts of "birth control" illegal and punishable as an offense, can only be approved by those who respect the Omnipotent will, and the time-hallowed traditions which date back to the very inception of the race.

CHAPTER IX
SEX DISEASES

The sex diseases are the same in both sexes, whether developed by direct or accidental infection. They are the greatest practical argument in favor of continence, morality and marriage in the sex relation.

GONORRHEA

Gonorrhea is a pus-discharging inflammation of the canal known as the *urethra*, which passing through the entire length of the organ, carries both the urine and the seminal fluid. It is caused by a venereal bacillus, the *gonococcus*. Under favorable conditions and with right treatment, gonorrhea may be cured, though violently painful, in fourteen days. Often the inflammation extends, becomes chronic and attacks other organs. This chronic gonorrhea often causes permanent contraction of the urethra, which leads to the painful retention of urine, catarrh of the bladder, and stone. Chronic gonorrhea, too, often ends in death, especially if the kidneys are attacked. A cured case of gonorrhea does not mean immunity from further attacks. New infections are all the more easily acquired. Gonorrhea has even more dangerous consequences in women than in men. The *gonococcus* bacilli infect all the inner female genital organs. They cause frequent inflammations and lead to growths in the belly. Women thus attacked usually are apt to be sterile; they suffer agonies, and often become chronic invalids. The child born of a gonorrheal mother, while passing through the infected genital organs, comes to life with infected eyelids. This is *Blennorrhea*, which may result in total blindness. Gonorrhea also causes inflammation of the joints, gonorrheal rheumatism, testicular inflammations which may lead to sterility. Some authorities claim that fully half the sterility in women is caused by gonorrheal infection of the Fallopian tubes. Gonorrheal infection of the eyes at birth is now prevented by first washing them in a saturated solution of boric acid, then treating them with a drop of weak silver solution.

SYPHILIS

Syphilis is a still more terrible venereal disease. It usually appears first in small, hard sores, hard chancres, on the sexual parts or the mouth. Then the syphilitic poison spreads throughout the whole body by means of the blood. After a few weeks it breaks out on the face or body. Its final cure is always questionable. Syphilis may lie dormant for years, and then suddenly become active again. It breaks out in sores on all parts of the body, often eats up the bone, destroys internal organs, such as the liver, causes hardening of the lungs, diseases of the blood vessels and eye diseases. Ulcers of the brain and nerve paralysis often result from it. One of its most terrible consequences is consumption of the spinal marrow and paralysis of the brain, or paresis. The first slowly hardens and destroys the spinal marrow, the second the brain. These diseases are only developed by previous syphilitics. As a rule they occur from 5 to 20 years after infection, usually 10 or 15 years after it. And they usually happen to persons who believed themselves completely cured. Consumption of the spinal marrow leads to death in the course of a few years of continual torture. Paralysis of the brain turns the sufferer into a human ruin, gradually extinguishing all mental and nervous functions, sentience, movement, speech and intellect.

One danger of syphilis is the fact that its true nature may be overlooked during the first period, because of the lack of pronounced symptoms. Its early sores may easily be mistaken for some skin affection. Mercury and other means are successful in doing away with at least the more noticeable signs of syphilis during the first and secondary stages. The modern medical treatment using mercury and Salvarsan (606) in alternation, has been very successful. It is claimed that by following it, syphilis may be totally cured if taken in hand during the first stage. The sores developed during the first two or three years of the disease are very infectious. In the case of a chronic syphilis of three or four years' standing, the sores as a rule are no longer infectious. It is possible, however, for a syphilitic of this description to bring forth syphilitic children, *without infecting his wife*. Such children either die at birth, or later, of this congenital syphilis. They may also die of spinal consumption or paresis between the ages of 10 and 20. The mortality of all syphilitic children is very great. In most cases, however, healthy children are born of the wedlock of *relatively cured* syphilitics, though they are often sterile. Young men who have had recourse to prostitutes, often inoculate their wives with gonorrhea or syphilis, and thus the plague is spread.

THE SOFT CHANCRE

The soft chancre is the third form of venereal disease (the hard chancre being the first stage of syphilis). It is the least dangerous of the venereal diseases, but unfortunately, relatively the one which occurs most seldom. When not complicated with syphilis, it appears locally. It is a larger or smaller sore feeding and growing on the genital organs.

VENEREAL DISEASE AN ADVOCATE OF CONTINENCE

The most tragic consequence of all venereal disease is the part it plays in the infection of innocent children, and innocent wives and mothers. Often a pure and chaste woman is thus deprived in the most cruel and brutal manner of the fruit of all her hopes and dreams of happiness. Similarly, a young man may find himself hopelessly condemned to a short life of pain and misery. He may also suffer from the knowledge that he has ruined the lives of those dearest to him. Venereal disease, syphilis in particular, emphasizes the *practical* value of continence—quite aside from its moral one—in a manner which cannot be ignored!

CHAPTER X
LOVE AND SEX

When we take under consideration the higher, truer love of one sex for the other, that is, an affection which is not simply a friendship, but has a sex basis, we realize that it may be a very noble emotion. There is no manner of doubt but that the normal human being feels a great need for love. Sex in love and its manifestation in the life of the soul is one of the first conditions of human happiness, and a main aim of human existence.

All know the tale of Cupid's arrow. A man falls in love with a face, a pair of eyes, the sound of a voice, and his affection is developed from this trifling beginning until it takes complete possession of him. This love is usually made up of two components: a sex instinct, and feelings of sympathy and interest which hark back to primal times. And this love, in its true sense, should stand for an affection purified from egoism.

When, among the lower animal forms we find individuals without a determined sex, egoism develops free from all restraint. Each individual creature devours as much as it can and feeding, together with propagation by division, "budding" or conjunction, makes up the total of its vital activities. It need do no more to accomplish the purpose of its existence. Even when propagation commences to take place by means of individual male and female parents, the same principle of egoism largely obtains. The spiders are typical instances of this: in their case the carrying out of the natural functions of the male spider is attended with much danger for him, owing to the fact that if he does not exercise the greatest care, he is apt to be devoured immediately afterward by his female partner, in order that no useful food matter may be lost. Yet even in the case of the spiders, the female spider already gives proof of a certain capacity for sacrifice where her young are concerned, at any rate for a short time after they have crept from the egg.

In animals somewhat higher in the creative scale, more or less powerful feelings of affection may develop out of their sex association. There is affection on the part of the male for his mate, and on the part of the female for her young. Often these feelings develop into a strong, lasting affection between the sexes, and years of what might be called faithful matrimonial union have been observed in the case of birds. This in itself is sufficient to establish the intimate relationship between love in a sex sense and love in a general sense. And even in the animal creation we find the same analogy existing between these feelings of sympathy and their opposites which occur in the case of human beings. Every feeling of attachment or sympathy existing between two individuals has a counterpart in an opposite feeling of discontent when the object of the love or attachment in question dies, falls sick, or runs away. This feeling of discontent may assume the form of a sorrow ending in lasting melancholy. In the case of apes and of certain parrots, it has been noticed that the death of a mate has frequently led the survivor to refuse nourishment, and die in turn from increasing grief and depression. If, on the other hand, an animal discovers the cause of the grief or loss which threatens it; if some enemy creature tries to rob it of its mate or little ones, the mixed reactive feeling of rage or anger is born in it, anger against the originator of its discontent. Jealousy is only a definite special form of this anger reaction.

A further development of the feeling of sympathy is that of duty. Every feeling of love or sympathy urges those who feel it to do certain things which will benefit the object of that love. A mother will feed her young, bed them down comfortably, caress them; a father will bring nourishment to the mother and her brood, and protect them against foes. All these actions, not performed to benefit the creature itself, but to help its beloved mate, represent exertion, trouble, the overcoming of danger, and lead to a struggle between egoism and the feeling of sympathy. Out of this struggle is born a third feeling, that of responsibility and conscience. Thus the elements of the human social feelings are already quite pronounced in the case of many animals, including those of love as well as sex.

In the human animal, speaking in general, these feelings of sympathy (love) and duty are strongly developed in the family connection; that is, they are developed with special strength in those who are most intimately united in sex life, in husband and wife and in children. Consequently the feelings of sympathy or love which extend to larger communal groups, such as more distant family connections, the tribe, the community, those speaking the same tongue, the nation, are relatively far weaker. Weakest of all, in all probability, is that general human feeling which sees a brother in every other human being and is conscious of the social duties owed him.

As regards man and wife, the relation of the actual sex instinct to love is often a very complicated one. In the case of man the sex feeling may, and frequently does exist independent of love in the higher sense; in the case of woman it is quite certain that love occurs far less seldom unaccompanied by the sex inclination. It is also quite possible for love to develop before the development of the sex feeling, and this often, in married life, leads to the happiest relationships.

The mutual adoration of two individuals, husband and wife, often degenerates into a species of egoistic enmity toward the remainder of the world. And this, in turn, in many cases reacts unfavorably upon the love the two feel for each other. Human solidarity, especially in this day, is already too great not to revenge itself upon the egotistical character of so exclusive a love. The real ideal of sex in love might be expressed as follows: A man and a woman should be induced to unite in marriage through genuine sex attraction and harmony of character and disposition. In this union they should mutually encourage each other to labor socially for the common good of mankind, in such wise that *they further their own mutual education and that of their children*, the beings nearest and dearest to them, *as the natural point of departure for helping general human betterment.*

If love in its relation to sex be conceived in this manner, it will purify it by doing away with its pettinesses and it is just into these pettinesses that the most honest and upright of matrimonial loves too often degenerate. The constructive work done in common by two human beings who, while they care lovingly for each other, at the same time encourage each other to strive and endure in carrying out the principles of right living and high thinking, will last. Love and marriage looked at from this point of view, are relatively immune from the small jealousies and other evil little developments of a one-sided, purely physical affection. It will work for an ever more ideal realization of love in its higher and nobler dispensations.

Real and true love is lasting. The suddenly awakened storm of sex affection for a hitherto totally unknown person can never be accepted as a true measure for love. This sudden surge of the sex feeling warps the judgment, makes it possible to overlook the grossest defects, colors all and everything with heavenly hues. It makes a man who is "in love," or two beings who are in love, mutually blind, and causes each to carefully conceal his or her real inward self from the other. This may be the case even when the feelings of both are absolutely honest, especially if the sex feeling is not paired with cool egoistic calculation. Not until the first storm of the sex feeling has subsided, when honeymoon weeks are over, is a more normal point of view regained. And then love, indifference, or hatred, as the case may be develops. It is for this reason that love at first sight is always dangerous, and that only a longer and more intimate acquaintance with the object of one's affection is calculated to give a lasting union a relatively good chance of turning out happily. One thing is worth bearing in mind. Woman invariably represents the conservative element in the family. Her emotional qualities, combined with wonderful endurance, always control her intellect more powerfully than is the case with man; and the feelings and emotions form the conservative element in the human soul.

www.ingramcontent.com/pod-product-compliance
Lightning Source LLC
Chambersburg PA
CBHW031255230426
43670CB00005B/202